Marketing
Made
Easy
for
Martial Arts
&
Self-Defense

Business Builder & Marketing Manual

Bonus of: 44 More Marketing Ideas

Researched and written by:
Earl O'Kuly

Edited by:
Tate Tatier

By The Book 4U Publishing
Brownstown, IL 62418
www.bythebook4u.com

ISBN: 978-0-9836908-1-8

Library of Congress control number: 2011939717

Library of Congress Headings:
Marketing
Advertising
Business Building
Communication
Martial Arts
Self-Defense
Business

Marketing Made Easy for Martial Arts & Self Defense
Business Builder and Marketing Manual

mar•ket•ing
noun
-the total of activities involved in the transfer of services from the seller to the buyer, including advertising and selling.

ad•ver•tis•ing
noun
-the act or practice of calling public attention to one's product, service, need, etc., especially by paid announcements in newspapers and magazines, over radio or television, on billboards, internet, etc.: advertising to get more customers; advertising to increase profits.

suc•cess
noun
-the favorable or prosperous termination of attempts or endeavors.

-the attainment of wealth, position, honors, or the like.

-a successful performance or achievement: The advertising was an instant success.

-a person or thing that is successful: The stylist was a great success in the community.

Also from By the Book 4U Publishing:

"By thinking outside of the diet . . . The Melee´ Method Way to Weigh Less" by E. Nelson and Tate Tatier
With most people not achieving their goal weight, and when over 85% of those that do gain their weight back, or more, this book shares the <u>secret</u> of how to beat those numbers. The Melee Method shows the 7 steps to success in achieving your goal weight, 2.5 ways to increase your metabolism and covers the top 10 reasons diets fail and ways to overcome them (but still not a diet book). It also has two bonus sections, one with 101 little ways to weigh less and medical reasons for weight gain. *(Available on Amazon.com)*

"HOH?" by Kate Carlson

A book on her experiences as a hard of hearing person, with chapters on coping skills and a final chapter on resources for the hearing impaired. *(Available on Amazon.com)*

"Devil at the Door" by Kate Carlson
This is the story of some of the trials and tribulations of Kate Carlson relating to what all hard of hearing people endure adjusting and adapting to this great change in their lives. Written in a light hearted and sometime humorous style it shares ways of coping with hearing impairment and it even gives the do's and don'ts for those who are 'hearing' people. This book is a must for those struggling with hearing impairment and a great book for those who interact with the hearing impaired. With a final chapter on resources this is a book to keep and use as a resource.
(Available on Amazon.com)

"By thinking outside of the box . . . The Audiologist's Business Manual for Success" by Earl O'Kuly and Tate Tatier
By thinking outside of the box, this manual starts with 57 ways to start your strategy of building your business. It then takes you down the road of connecting with others, then closing the sale to meet their needs. The final section is a fun section to open your mind to the possibilities of your business and your life. Filled with 'black gold', nuggets and gems, it is a resource to take your practice, your business, to a higher level.
(Available on Amazon.com)

The Stylist and Salon Handbook for Keeping Customers and Making Money" by Earl O'Kuly and Tate Tatier

Customers buy from and are more loyal to those they like and trust.

You will learn Three significant lessons from this book:
1. How to connect with people and get them to like and trust you.
2. Twenty-one ways to build your clientele.
3. Learn what business you are really in . . . and why it is important.

All it takes to create the volume of business you are seeking is that one great idea to take hold. Inside, you will find a great deal more than just one of those ideas. This book makes dollars and sense.

I've surveyed over one hundred people, both men and women ranging from high school seniors to senior citizens, in order to bring you the answers that will help you build your clientele and increase your income. I've visited salons and talked to people, like you, who like what they do and want to make more money doing it. This book will give the tools you need to be successful in the career you love.

Marketing Made Easy for Martial Arts and Self-Defense

Set the Table of Success - Contents

Business Builder & Marketing Manual

Warning:

1. Please use common sense when following the information in this book. All promises, implied or otherwise, are made on a general level and may be different for each person or business on an individual level.

2. Refrain from anything that you see or feel is harmful or detrimental to you and/or your business because ultimately you are the person responsible for your results

4. Use the information in this book wisely. Your situation may not apply to everything written.

5. No results can be guaranteed. The authors nor the publisher can be held responsible for your use or results.

Foreword and Forward Towards Success

Ask questions to turn your dreams into reality!

What marketing and advertising have you used in an attempt to promote your business? Incentives to students for referrals? Newspaper ads? Billboards? And you just didn't get the results you wanted, did you?

Do you believe in cause and effect? In reasons and results? If you do then this book is for you. It is about making things happen positively! It is about building your business.

This book is for Martial Arts and Self-Defense Schools that have been in business at least a year and that have the capacity for growth. If you meet these two criteria, please read on.

What you are going to learn is how to build a track for yourself, where you want your business to go, then you will learn how to build a track for others to use to help you, and them, achieve a common goal. I am a firm believer that others want to help, they just don't know how.

12

You will learn to sell the sizzle, not the steak. That means you will learn to find the benefits of your product that each individual wants then translate that into target marketing, sometimes known as niche marketing).

In conjunction with that you will learn to put in reality with the 80/20 rule. A large key to success is that you do not need a fantastic product, but follow the example of Ray Kroc and McDonalds. McDonalds doesn't have the greatest hamburgers, but they were one of the first to market convenience, cleanliness and trust. You will find out how to find marketing triggers.

How big can you grow? That is up to you. The key ideas in this manual are not expensive, however some of the advertising will cost money. You will see ways in the manual to make your advertising more effective. You will need to decide on an advertising budget. Then it depends on how wisely you spend your money and your time. However, the basics are here for you to double (or more) your business over the next eighteen months or less if you diligently work at making your business grow!

You will learn the difference between marketing and advertising. You will learn how to constantly market and how to wisely advertise. You will learn what advertising mediums work best for most schools like yours.

Albert Einstein said, "Finding the right answer is usually a function of asking the right question."

You will find a lot of questions in this book. They are made to make you think. How you answer some of them will make a huge difference in your success.

Chapter 1

The basics and being prepared for an influx of new business

Are you really prepared for new business? I did consulting for a business that claimed they were running at 40% capacity and wanted help to market their services to fill the remaining capacity. I had him do one thing while I was going to research his business to build a marketing plan. However, he found out he was running at 80% capacity when he couldn't handle all of the business brought in from this one effort!

Do you have the floor space for additional students?

Do you have people who can help when you have new students?

Do you have enough showers and lockers? Do you have separate showers and lockers for men and women? This is something to seriously consider, especially if you go after the women's market to build your business.

Do you have enough parking? This is critical because many a business has stalled or failed completely due to lack and ease of parking.

These questions should make you think. However do not be too optimistic with your numbers. If you make classes too large people will be too crowded and you will lose more than you gain. It is better to have more smaller classes than to try to handle too many students at a time.

How about your building's outer appearance? Does it look inviting? One of the best highlights to capture the attention of people driving by was a self-defense school that had a neon strip around the plate glass windows. It was an eye catcher without being gaudy.

When your prospective students enter your school, what do they see? Is it inviting or intimidating?

Do you have pictures of your students succeeding?

Do you have letters from your students that give your school a commendation or endorsement?

Is it clean and neat?

Does it have an odor? You might want to consider in investing in an ionizer to use to eliminate unwanted smells.

Do you have brochures by the door? You should have brochures for each marketing niche you want to target. They should be quality. Do your brochures show the benefits of attending your school? Are they in a holder that looks professional?

Does your stationery look professional? Does it have a benefit on it somewhere? The benefit can be as simple as 'Self-defense and more . . .' Remember that it is an extension of your business and it is all someone who has not been to your school sees. Right or wrong, they relate this directly to how they perceive your school.

You do have business cards, don't you? Consider each of these to be a soldier and arm them accordingly. They should match your stationary, however they need to have at least two benefits on them. You might even want to print up cards for each marketing niche you are pursuing. Cards can be powerful! They aren't any more than informational if all they have on them is your school's name, address and phone number. Your competitor's cards are probably like that, right?

So dare to be different. Make them work for you. Use them wisely and leave them everywhere!

Summary

Are you prepared for an influx of new students?

Is your building's outer appearance inviting?

Is there ample parking?

Is it within a reasonable distance?

Is the inside appearance acceptable for new business?

Is it clean?

Does it have an odor?

What does the appearance convey?

Do you have letters of commendation and thank you cards and letters posted?

Do you have pictures of activities?

How is your personal appearance? Are you clean and neat?

Does your appearance convey your school?

Are your stationary and business cards professional and do they match?

Do you have attention grabbing headlines?

Do you have a brochure and business card for each niche you are wanting for your school?

Do you have a rack of quality looking brochures? Are they truly professional looking? Do they have attention grabbing headlines?

Note: I will be going over each of these again and much more in helping you build your business.

Chapter 2

Know your markets, work your markets

You have heard that knowledge is power. Well it is true! But it is only power if you use it. Do you know who your competitors are? How they advertise? What they charge? How many students they have? How their school is different from yours? What, within the differences, can you capitalize on to promote, to market your school to gain market share?

Answer these questions and you will not only know your competition's strengths and weaknesses, but you will know more about your own school. What makes you different? Can you use this as a selling point to get students to your school over your competitor's school? Do they use coupons? Can you make a better coupon? You need to know what you have to offer that you can use as a benefit to have potential customers perceive you as a better choice.

Now, do you know why you lose students? What kind of turnover do you have? What is the ratio of how many new students stay versus now many drop out? Use groups of five to calculate this. What do you spend on advertising to get students? Calculate it on what the cost is for students who stay. Again figure this on a per student cost, then again use a group of five students to calculate the cost.

Using round numbers lets use an example of spending $5,000.00 for advertising last year and with that the school was able to get 90 responses and from that get 50 new students. Out of that 50, only 10 are still attending on a regular basis. Now we divide 10 into $5,000.00 and find that it cost $500.00 to get each new student. (Note, the cost is actually higher when you consider that you do not have any cost when a current student refers a friend or relative.)

Now let's calculate what each student is worth. For simplicity, let's not count any students who attended less than a year because when you factor in your overhead, you don't make much money on those students. (I am going to show you how to retain more of these students, so continue reading.)

Again, for simplicity, let's say you charge $50.00 a month, they would have to stay 10 months for you to recoup your advertising cost. This doesn't include your other expenses for a new student, to include your overhead. With this in mind you need a new student to attend two years at a minimum to really make any money and it is actually 3 years for the student to be a part of your profit!

Can you see why it is more profitable to keep students you have signed up to stay longer? The above calculations should show you that you need to find out what your costs are. Can you get more than $50.00 per month per student? Can you lower advertising costs? (I will cover this later in the book.) You need to know this information to make better decisions.

I say this because I want you to see the opportunity in trying to bring these students back. It costs considerably less to get these dropouts back into the fold than it does to get new students through advertising. The survey for the dropouts (see it at the end of the chapter) will tell you why they left and usually what it will take to get them to return. Sweeten the deal with a coupon and emphasize the reason they joined in the first place plus mention some of the benefits they will get by coming back and with each one that returns your cash flow has just gone up!

You should also survey your current students to gather information. What they like, what they don't like, and what they would change. Often just giving people an opportunity to express their ideas and opinions goes a long way towards making them happy.

Another area to look at when get the surveys back is what age group is predominant? What gender is predominant? What income bracket is predominate? What race is predominant? Is there a geographic area that is predominate? Is there more than one specific area? The answers to these questions will show you what your base group is made of and opportunities within these groups. You know you are succeeding with this type of group and should pursue it.

However, the flip side to this is to see what markets are wide open. If you have mostly males as students this means you have a big potential for building women's classes. How about age? I will bet the potential for senior's classes is very big. Most schools do not have many children. If you were to build children's classes, guess what? You can then develop a mother's class and /or a parent's class. This is known as niche marketing, finding areas that can be exploited for the growth of your school.

24

Do you see the power of knowledge gleaned from these surveys? It can open your eyes to current problems, current opportunities, and major areas to pursue to build your business.

Part of your market analysis is to evaluate your area of business. Are you in a business or a residential area? Is there plenty of parking available for new students if you expand your classes. How many local newspapers are there? Do you have a local cable channel? Is there a local radio station? Are there large businesses in your area? The answers to these questions will give you valuable knowledge to use when considering expanding your current student size, when considering paid advertising and when considering what medium to use for the best results.

Sample Survey for PRIOR STUDENTS:

Name: Age:

Occupation:

How   far   do   you   live   from   the   school?

How far do you work from the school?

What   did   you   like   best   about   the   school?

What did you like least about the school?

If you could change one thing about the school, what would you change?

What caused you to stop attending the school?

On a scale of 1 to 5, one being very poor and 5 being very good, please rate the following. Circle your choice.

1. Parking availability   1 2 3 4 5
1. External appearance   1 2 3 4 5
1. Inside appearance   1 2 3 4 5
1. Equipment   1 2 3 4 5
1. Locker room and shower   1 2 3 4 5

Chapter 3

Signs convey a message, what do your signs say?

Signage does make a difference!

Can people driving by read your signs easily? Does it catch their eyes to make them want to read it? Do you have a portable or changeable sign you can use to post benefits or special training? If you do, and you should, you must make sure that you change it weekly. You should never use the same one for more than a month. If your city has ordinances on signage, don't give up. Did you know that if you put a sign on a car or truck and park it out front, they can't stop you?

I know of a person who has a service business in a strip mall and his business was on the side away from the street. On top of that, the city he was in had very restrictive signage laws. People driving along the street seldom saw the small sign he was allowed to display by the city. He tried to fight the law, but he lost. So he went out and bought a pickup truck and had a large sign placed in the bed of the truck. He parked this next to the street and his business picked up dramatically.

I used this same idea for a printing franchise who was about to go under because of restrictive signage laws in his city. He started with an inexpensive trailer and a 4x8 sign. His business soon picked up because he was in a high traffic area. He was able to purchase delivery vans which he also placed signage on, and when not in use, he had parked in other busy locations. This not only saved his business, it gave him the profits he needed to expand and grow.

Please make sure you grasp this and see the potential. This is an unbelievable business builder. As a matter of fact, you should have at a minimum four signs. This would allow you to post each of them three times a year, four months apart so they do not become boring. Each one should have a different 'hook' (more on this later) to meet different potential customer's interest.

By the way, these signs don't have to be placed in the back of a truck. They can be written on the side of a truck or a van. Using magnetic signs make it quick and easy to change signs. You can even place signs on a luggage rack on top of a car and park it next to the street. There is another awesome way to take advantage of these signs and that is to park the vehicle at a busy intersection or at a busy mall. The key is to get an attention getting headline above your school's name to get people to come into your business!

Hopefully you are on a busy street and can take advantage of a large front window. Four foot by four foot signs are inexpensive and a great way to post promotions. Remember to make a great attention grabbing headline on it! What makes a great headline? Something that grabs the person's attention and motivates them to take action, which in this case is to come into your business.

Note: This is called copywriting. Some of the top copywriting words and phrases are: free, limited time, special offer, lose weight, learn.

Neon signs are attention grabbers. At a minimum you should have one, large and bright, that says OPEN. Make sure you purchase one with a switch that you can use every other week that causes the sign to flash on and off every 15 seconds. It is worth the extra money to have a sign that you can use to alternate to keep it fresh for traffic going by your school. This is so people who drive by on a daily basis do not get used to just seeing a lighted open sign. Think variety!

Summary

Signs can bring in new business quickly.

If you have large store front windows facing a busy street, take advantage with window signs.

If you are not close to the street, use a pickup truck, van, trailer, even your car to post signs next to the street. Remember also to park them at busy intersections or busy malls sometimes to let people know about your school.

MAKE SURE ALL SIGNS HAVE AN ATTENTION GETTING HEADLINE THAT GRABS INTEREST AND MOTIVATES THE READER TO COME TO YOUR SCHOOL!

Marketing Made Easy for Martial Arts & Self Defense
Business Builder and Marketing Manual

Chapter 4

If you give them a track to run on, you can get them to go where you want them to go!

The oldest and best way to build you business is word-of-mouth. The best way to get new students is word-of-mouth. Satisfied students telling friends, family and coworkers how much they like your school and how they benefitted from attending is the best way to get referrals.

You are probably getting some referrals this way. Yet you know the potential for even more is there!

You have probably offered free classes or discounts as an incentive to get your students to send referrals. It probably didn't work as well as you would have liked though, did it? What went wrong?

That question brings us to one of the foundations of this book . . . give people a track to run on and they will go where you need them to go. The best way to explain this concept is with a true story. As they were walking down the hall to leave, the sound of a small child screaming for help came to them, however over that sound was the sound of the father as he punisher her. Their small child looked up at them and asked, "Can't we help her? Can't we do something?" And the parents answered with a no, and they walked on; they went to the beach and had their picnic. However, when they returned home there was an ambulance parked out front and the attendants were loading the dead body of the small girl into it. The police were taking away the father.

When questioned as to why they didn't help, their answer was they didn't know what to do. They wanted to help, but didn't know what to do. The sequel to this story is that anytime you hear on the radio an 800 number to call if you see child abuse, it is because this family decided to build a track for others so they would know what to do, how to help if they see or hear child abuse. Now thousands of people are informed, have a track to run on because of this. It will not bring the little girl back, but has helped hundreds of other children since then.

I feel that people do want to help, but so many times they don't know what to do. People are basically good, they often just need a track to run on and sometimes an incentive to get on and stay on track. The above story is not about business, it is about life and an insight to people.

So how do you build a track? First, do you have the surveys done? You see, you need a track to run on before you can build a track for others. You will need to know where you are and where you want to go before you can ask for help from others. Not having a plan is like asking for directions when you don't know where you want to go.

Talking to your former students will let you know what you need to fix to keep more students from dropping out. You should have had some students return because of the coupon you sent with the survey. You did enclose a coupon, didn't you?

The surveys from your current students should give you the makeup of your current group. Were there any surprises? Did you find a lot of common traits? You should!

Most Martial Arts and Self Defense Schools have been built around a common group. This will be your core group to build upon. You will find that these students will, for the most part, tend to bring in students like themselves as referrals. That is unless you help them expand their vision to see others outside their 'blinders' as potential students.

An example of this would be to give them copies of the   , Appendix A, at the back of this manual. Ask them to show it to women they know. (However, before you do this, please finish the book so you handle this correctly.)

The key to successful marketing, the key to getting referrals from your students is to give them a track to run on. If they know what you want and expect them to do, and you show them how to do it, in essence, give them a track to run on, you will see amazing results compared to the referrals they have sent so far.

However before you become too excited about this concept, let me bring a reality check into this. There is a rule called the 80/20 rule, also known at the Pareto Principle after the person who brought it to light. This principle states that 20% of your people will generate 80% of your referrals and 80% of your people will only do 20% of your referrals.

A quick analogy would be for you to look in your clothes closet. Most people wear 20% of their clothes 80% of the time and 80% of their clothes only 20% of the time. To bring this home, think how often you wear your favorite t-shirt or sweatshirt instead of that really nice dress shirt.

What this means to your plan to build your business is that not everyone will cooperate even when you give them a track to run on. That is the bad news.

The good news is that with a track to run on you can expect 20% of your students to do a better job, a much better job, and you will see some success from the other 80% of your students. What you should see is the 20% send you three or more referrals each. So if you have 100 students and 20% of them bring in three or more referrals that would be 60 or more referrals and if the other 80% were to only average 1/2 referral each, you would end up with at least one hundred referrals.

Before you go any further though, please make sure you have done the surveys with both your current students and those who have dropped out Make sure you take care of any complaints. And don't just rely on the surveys, you should walk around your place of business to make sure it looks good both inside and out. Do you have brochures and are they professional and laid out professionally? Do you have a plan, once a prospect shows up, to get them to sign up? Are you prepared to get them to commit to 90 days to give your school a valid test (plus to get them into the habit of attending)? Are you prepared to take on a large group of new students if this goes as planned?

If you have taken care of all of the above, and then some, to make this work you are going to have to do three things successfully:

1. present this to your current students.
2. show them how to make referrals using the cards and the article, Appendix A (this gives them a track to run on).
3. have incentives (prizes) that will motivate them to action.

This will get referrals from your students. How well you present, deliver and follow-up will dictate your degree of success.

The first part, how to present it, can be done in a number of ways:

-strictly as a contest

-let them know in a straight forward manner you need and want their help to build your business

-as a way to maintain present prices (as in that if you don't get more students you will have to raise your prices)

-a combination of the above

I recommend you use the combination of the first two. Tell your students you need their help to build your business. To make it worthwhile and challenging you are going to have a contest where they can all win and the only losers will be the non-participants.

This is probably the hardest part. It needs to be done without begging for their help, yet it must not seem like an order. Make sure to thank them in advance for their help.

The next step is to show them how to make a referral and to make it easy for them to make a referral. Also show them how they will get credit for a referral.

This is easily done by giving them a 3x5 card to pass out. these cards have a multiple purpose. They give the students a track to run on. All they do is write the person's name on the card, their name on the card, then give it to that person to bring to you to talk to you about what it can mean to them to join your school. These cards should also have printed on them an opportunity and a benefit to attend your school. And finally, it has your student's name on it for tracking their successes in the contest.

You will find three examples of cards at the end of this chapter. You can use any one you want or pick and print two different ones. You can use these as they are or you can write your own. Some suggestions:

-make sure your schools phone number and address are on them

-make sure the referrals name is on the card

-make sure the student's name is on the card

-if you location needs a map to find it, have one printed on the back of the card

-when having them printed you can have your signature imprinted to personalize it

-use colored paper to grab the attention of the recipient

-print five thousand cards (there is a reason for this and it really doesn't cost that much to have them printed, i.e., the more you have printed the less expensive they are per card)

After giving your presentation to your students, you should give each student ten cards. If you opted to print two different cards then give each person five of each type. Make sure they see all of the cards you had printed!

Tell them if they would like more they can get them from you personally. Keep all of the extra cards in your office and make sure you pass them out personally. Never leave them out in the open. There are two psychological elements to this. Subconsciously you are keying the importance of the contest AND by showing them all of the cars you are showing them that you expect more from them.

Now is a good time to show them the article, Appendix A, you want them to use to help you to recruit women. Tell them of your plans, whether it is to have coed classes or specific classes for women, and then give them a copy of the article to use in conjunction with the cards. This where you might want to use two different sets of cards as I mentioned earlier. Use one for the general public and one to recruit more women.

The third area of this program is crucial. You need to choose the prizes that will motivate them and keep them on track. You can add free classes and/or discounts to your students for their referrals, but you probably have tried that before and found it is not a great incentive. You should, however, use these in conjunction with a prize, but the prize itself should be **tangible**.

Let's talk about what not to use. I've seen businesses give away televisions sets. Think about what you want to offer because when you think about it, most people have a television, often more than one. They usually have DVD players. A dinner at a restaurant is nice, but it only lasts one night, then it is over and gone.

You might want to try something with your Martial Arts and Self Defense School that has a martial arts theme like nun chucks with free classes thrown in. However, what I have seen that works well is t-shirts, sweatshirts and silk looking jackets. Note: They also have the **added benefit of being free advertising for your school when they are worn in public!** Double bang for your bucks!

An example of a contest using these would be a free t-shirt for three new students and a nice jacket for double that. If someone sends you six new students, make sure you give them both the t-shirt and the jacket. Remember to go for quality. Spend the extra few dollars, because you want your students to wear these AND you want them to be a powerful representation of your school. Think of how many people will see the name of your school when your students wear these items and think of the impact top quality will have versus whatever you get cheap.

In talking about quality, the jackets, should you decide to use them, should be a class act! Even if you were to spend $100.00 per jacket (and you won't need to), figure out what you will make the first month on six new students, then add a second month and a third month. That total should have you realizing, wouldn't you like to give away a lot of jackets? And if someone sends you enough new students to earn a second t-shirt and jacket, give these to them with a smile! That is six more students and once again, free advertising when your students wear them. A side note, never, never, never give away a jacket to a student unless they have earned it. It is a quick way to devalue the jacket, the contest and your integrity.

Can you see the importance of having the right prizes to motivate students? People want to help, but they need to know how, and they need to be motivated. More importantly, they want to win! You need to show them they can. Then make it as easy as possible for them to do this.

Make a big show out of it when someone does win. The prize should be awarded in a group setting. The person should be made to feel as though they have accomplished something special. Another way to recognize those people who earn a prize is to put their name on a signboard marked WINNERS! Don't not just tack it to a bulletin board or tape it to the wall. Make it special and make sure it is prominent so everyone coming into the school will see it.

One last thing: One hundred referrals mean nothing if few to none become students. You need to have a great presentation for referrals. You need to sign them up while they are there. If possible, accept credit cards to make it easier for them. If they need to think about it and they leave, the odds are you have lost them.

It is not the scope of this manual to teach you sales. It is to show you techniques you can use to market your business. However, I highly recommend you get a book on sales or attend classes on sales because you need to be able to do this to build your business.

Last, but definitely not least, when you get a new student, please get a commitment from him or her. You need to get a verbal commitment. You need to get a written commitment. Get them to commit to 90 days. Tell them if at the end of 90 days, if they don't feel better health wise and feel better about themselves then they should quit. Because you know and I know, if they hang in there for 90 days, they are going to feel better! You need to call them if they don't show up. Give them only one excuse for not being there, death . . . theirs. (Put this to them humorously, but with emphasis to make a point of how important it is to them to make this commitment to change their life.)

Everyone has quit something in their lives, tell them not to let something as important as this be one of them. Tell them to come even if they are tired. Tell them to come even if they don't feel like it, because once they are there they will feel better!

SAMPLE OF 3x5 CARDS

#1

Name of school, 123 Street, Any town, State, Zip
Phone number

Dear _____, (referral prints their name here)

You are cordially invited for a free session.   Learn self
defense, self-control, and as a bonus lose weight and feel
great!

Please come by,   Sincerely,

_____   _____

Instructor   Current Student

#2

Name of school, 123 Street, Any town, State, Zip
Phone number

Dear _____, (referral prints their name here)

If you have ever thought you might like to check out a self defense school NOW is your opportunity. We invite you to come by and observe or even better, bring sweats and participate in one of our classes.

You can learn self defense, self-control, and as a bonus lose weight, having more energy and feeling great!

Please come by,   Sincerely,

_____   _____

Instructor   Current Student

#3

Name of school, 123 Street, Any town, State, Zip
Phone number

Dear _____, (referral prints their name here)

You can learn self-defense!   To prove it, all you need to do
is come by for a free session (wear sweats) and give us a try.
Why not?   It's free and you just might have fun.

Please come by,   Sincerely,

_____   _____

Instructor   Current Student

SAMPLE SLOGANS FOR JACKETS

'WE HAVE ALL THE RIGHT MOVES'

'WE HAVE THE BEST PUT DOWNS IN TOWN'

'KICKING IT INTO HIGH GEAR'

'Learn to say NO . . . and MEAN IT!'

'MOVING IN A NEW DIRECTION'

'KNOW FEAR   NO FEAR!'

'BELTS MAKE A DIFFERENCE!'

'BELTS HAVE CLASS'

Self Control, Self Defense & Self Esteem
All wrapped up in a belt!

I'M IN A WHOLE NEW CLASS!'

'Taking Art to a new level!'

Remember to put your school's name and address under the one you choose to use. If you really want to get your name out there, put your school's name on the chest of the t-shirt or jacket with the slogan and the name of the school on the back.   BE BOLD!

If you find a slogan you really like, you can use it on brochures and other literature to help you get attention and build your business.

Summary

Word of mouth advertising is the best, so give your students a track to run on.

-Make 3x5 cards for them to pass out.
-Give them each a copy of the article for the women they know.
-Have great prizes!
-Keep the cards secure and hand them out personally.
-Post the names of the winners.
-Recognize and praise the winners.
-Give them reasons to refer new students, besides the prizes:
> -More body types to learn on.
> -More personalities to learn about.
> -They will have new people they can help train, and remind them they learn and retain more when they help train.

-Get commitments from new students . . . Verbally and in Writing!   Call them when they don't show up.   This one idea will make dollars and sense for you.

Tips for business building:
-Accept credit cards.
-Have attention getting headlines on everything.

-Get a commitment from new students.

-Have current students write up testimonials.

-Post letters from students who have commended your school.

-Post letters from students who have had to use their training. (I was attacked in the hallway of an apartment complex and although I had less than a year of training I was able to take down my attacker.) When students tell you about these incidents ask them to write them up and post them.

Stories are a great way to share you and your school and to make it memorable. Stories can also build interest and motivate a person to come by so you can get them to sign up.

Chapter 6

Putting niches to work for you.

Have you ever thought about what business you are in? Martial Arts? Self Defense? Both?

Please, take your blinders off! Yes, you are in both of the above, but if you look around you will see you do a lot more for your students:

Are they more physically fit?
Have they lost weight?
Have they gained self confidence?
How about self control?
Are you in the training business?

You probably answered yes to many of the above, but you are scratching your head as to what these questions mean. Have you ever heard of niche marketing? Niche marketing, sometimes called target marketing, is finding an area to market to. You are doing it now. You niche has been promoting your martial arts and/or self defense. What you need to do now is expand from that market using it as a base. Plus when you do this you are also going to be doing networking. This is working with other people and businesses to refer potential students to your school.

However, you should be able to reciprocate by referring people to them or showing them a benefit for referring people to your school.

Let's look at a possible niche for you to do networking in: weight loss. Three reasons for choosing this one: first it is always in the top three New Year's Resolutions in the United States which opens a huge market, secondly most experts agree weight loss programs work much better when they include an exercise program, and thirdly almost every town has at least two and often many more different types of weight loss centers you can offer to work with.

If the people need to exercise in conjunction with their diet, don't you agree they should come to you so that they not only lose weight, but also, as a bonus, learn self defense! This makes sense, dollars and sense, doesn't it? Getting two benefits for the price of one sounds great, plus everyone likes to save money, don't they?

If you like this niche then your first step is to go to the nearest bookstore or library and read up on dieting. Take notes and learn some of the terms.

You might want to send someone to the local weight centers to gather information and brochures for you.   You can get a lot of information about each center from the web also.

What benefits can you offer the weight loss centers?   Once you know the industry, the first thing you learn is they have a large dropout rate. You can show them that by combining your classes with theirs, you can help with self esteem and self confidence which will help with 'sticking to it.' Second, you can show that experts agree that dieting and exercise go together and that you are willing to give each of them a discount to sign up and get their exercise with you.   Win-wins make dollars and sense for both you and for them!!!

Their clients win by losing unwanted pound, feeling better, and as a bonus learn self defense. You give them a regimented exercise program as part of your training.   The extra effort you will need to do is to help them track their progress. This in turns helps keep them in the weight loss program AND your school so it is worth the effort. Also, it makes them feel special because you are taking an interest in them and their problem. Please note, once again, that the best thing you can do when they are talking about joining is to get them to commit to attending for 90 days no matter what. Tell them up front that they cannot make an educated decision without trying it at least that length of time. Get a commitment!!!

Armed with all of the knowledge you have put together, you need to setup a meeting with a weight loss center. You goal is for them to allow you to talk to their groups about using your school as their fitness program in conjunction with their diet program.

If they say yes, go for it! If possible videotape your presentation or at the very least, audiotape it. You want to critique yourself. You want to get better each time you do this, plus it helps you remember what you did right, the questions asked, and where you need to improve. Your goal with these groups is to get the individuals to attend your classes. Show them as many benefits as possible: weight loss, better health, lower blood pressure, more energy, and the bonus . . . self defense.

Another niche to look at when your marketing business is age. What ages are the majority of your students? Most schools are predominately in the 20's and 30's with some older students and comprised mostly of males.

This opens your school for more seniors, kids and females. So how about opening up a class for kids, then it makes sense to have a mom's class or a parent's class. Doesn't this make dollars and sense for you?

Before you start with moms or a parents class you might want to start with a kid's class (unless you want to do a discount program and bring both groups on board simultaneously). First you need to decide what age group of kids you want to work with (or start classes with different age groups). There are grade school, middle school and high school ages (college students can attend with adults). Work one group at a time unless you can have experienced students helping because these groups can be a handful until you get them initiated to your program.

Where do you find kids? The schools. Will the schools just let you come in and tout your school?

Probably not unless you do it as teaching kids how to avoid being picked up by strangers and you just mention your school in passing and maybe have it listed as the sponsor on a handout. This involves a lot of preparation but can be well worth it.

You need to become an expert on child safety. You should have a brochure printed up with safety tips for children. Make sure it has your school's name and phone number on it, however, the bulk and the theme should be on teaching/sharing with the children how to be safe. You need to get a lot of outside feedback on this because it not only has to be principal and teacher approved, it has to be mom approved to pass muster to be passed out.

Your number one goal is to be able to give a safety/martial arts presentation to an assembly of the school's students. If you have one that is truly geared towards safety, is geared to the age level of the students and has some humor, you have a small chance at getting in the door. However, your backup plan is to, at a minimum, be able to get the brochures passed out.

Another way to get your brochures to the students and their mothers is the PTA. You will find it is much easier to get in front of them to give a presentation. The downside is this group is a small population of the parents so try very hard to get into the school itself.

Note: You will have to have two brochures: one teaching/sharing child safety, and the second touting the benefits of your school. They will learn how to avoid a dangerous situation and what to do if grabbed in one brochure. Your other brochure will let them know they will learn self defense and they will learn self discipline if they attend your school. Attending will also help build their self esteem. It will help them become physically fit. It will keep them from the television. And to add a bit of humor: It will keep them out of your hair for awhile. Use two brochures, one on safety, one on the benefits of attending your school.

Before I end this chapter, let's look at some the niches you might want to consider pursuing:
-grade school age students
-middle school age students
-high school age students
-college students
-senior citizens
-females
-people who want to lose weight
-people who want to become physically fit
-people who want more self confidence
-couples classes
-family classes
-mom classes
-large businesses in your area (this can be as simple as a flyer on their bulletin board offering a discount for employees)
-organizations and clubs

Hopefully this has opened your eyes to the idea of niche marketing to build your business. Within that, you should now realize you do a lot more for your students that just martial arts and self defense.

Summary

Find and target niche markets!

Women
> Use the article to get women interested
> Advertise specifically for this market

Grade school and high school students
> Offer to give a demonstration to the students
> Offer a safety brochure to the students
> Contact the PTA

College students
> Advertise on campus
> Use flyers
> Use door hangers

Do a discount for moms and kids combined

Network with weight loss centers

Network with police departments

Large businesses - give a discount to employees

Civic organizations - give members a discount

Chapter 6

Follow you money!

Go through your personal and business checkbooks. Make a list of all the places you do business. At these places you are their customer. I am sure they like the money you spend at their businesses.

So if you were to ask them to let you put a flyer up, or a stand with brochures where their customers can see them, just for a month, the odds are they will say yes. Make sure to ask them to share these with their employees.

Remember, you should always give them a reason (benefit to them) for helping you. Keeping your business is one, but you need to add to that. A double win for you is to offer to buy refrigerator magnets with not only your school's name and number on it, but their number also (this works even better when you can get three or four businesses to let you do this). In conjunction with the businesses information, to get people to take them and put them on their refrigerator, or wherever they place these, you will put all of the area's important contact numbers. This will include, but is not limited to, fire department, police department, water department, ambulance, hospital, etc. This should get you an additional month, and possibly an ongoing spot at multiple locations. Make sure they let you place your school's brochures along with the magnets.

You are not limited to the businesses you do business with. Stop in at busy places to meet the owners and learn more about them and their business. Be honest. Be sincere. Tell them part of the reason you stopped in was to see if they would be interested in networking with you, and if they would be interested in letting you put your brochures in their store/business. You might even have a place where they can put the name of their business on your brochure and if they send you a certain number of new students you will give them six months of free classes. Talk to them to find out what works best, what will make this a win-win for both of you. Note: Often just making the offer works wonders. And if they take you up on it, see if you can interest them in earning a t-shirt and a jacket!

Summary

Go to places where you do business personally and ask them to allow you to place brochures on their counter and/or a flyer on their bulletin board. This works especially well at restaurants, grocery stores, even dry cleaners.

This can even work at the business to business level with: printers, office supplies, janitorial supplies, equipment suppliers.

Consider networking with a number of businesses and printing up refrigerator magnets with all of your businesses names and phone numbers and then make it a 'need to have' by placing a number of important local area phone numbers on it.

You can add coupons with the brochures (which should have attention getting headlines) to get people interested and to come to you.

Chapter 9

Advertising: TV - Radio - Newspaper

Marketing is all of the ways you can use to build and promote your business. Advertising is usually paid for, is usually persuasive and identifies the sponsor. Don't believe everything you hear about advertising.

There are always numbers about the number of people each type of advertising reaches. Television touts the number of people watching; radio talks about the number of listeners, and newspapers write about number of people receiving their paper. Then all of these talk about frequency, i.e., how often or how many times your ad runs. Now I am going to tell you the rest of this story, should you choose to use any one of these, there is a magic number, seven, that you need to be aware of because that is how many times you need to ensure the majority of their audience either sees, hears or reads your message. There is another factor in this and that is none of these three are inexpensive. Just the opposite, to hit the maximum number of people with the required frequency you will need to spend some big bucks. If you have the money, then this can be an awesome way to spend your money. Of the three, radio, using drive time with max frequency is a good bet for your business. Second choice would be in a newspaper, a big ad, lower side of a right hand page would be the best way to spend your money remembering you have to run it and run it and run it.

Sample radio ad:

"It doesn't matter . . . it doesn't matter whether you want to lose weight, look better, feel more confident or just take back control of your life. You can talk about it, you can hide from it, you can even run from it, but nothing happens until you decide you are ready . . . when you decide to take control. And when you are ready, I will be there for you. I don't promise it will be easy . . . **what I do promise is when you give me 90 days <u>you</u> will look better, <u>you</u> will feel better, <u>you</u> will be more confident! Will it be worth it? Come by, try it for 90 days and then . . . when you look in the mirror, when you walk down the street, you decide! I'm Master _____ and when you are ready . . . I will be here for you, I promise!** Announcer: You can find (name of your school or academy) at (your school's location)."

Sample newspaper ad:

'What are you waiting for?

Really, what are you waiting for?

Whether you want to lose weight, look better, feel more confident or just take back control of your life you need to ask yourself why?   Why not now?

Give me 90 days and <u>you</u> will look better, <u>you</u> will feel better, <u>you</u> will be more confident, I promise!

I'm Master _____ and when you are ready . . . I will be here for you, I promise. (name of your school or academy) (your school's location)'

You have to decide if you want to invest the money required for any these venues.

However, before leaving newspapers, let me share another way to take advantage of their readership. I had a client that used inserts in his local newspaper. These can be the size of a full sheet of paper, however his were the size of a half sheet of paper, on card stock, four color. Note: Most newspapers will print these for a fee.

He sent these out as a coupon, once a year at tax time, to take advantage of people getting their tax refunds. It was his number one pull, year after year. Something for you to consider, especially if money is a factor in making your decision.

Chapter 8

Advertising: Yellow Pages - Web Pages

Have you been contacted concerning the Yellow Pages, Yellow Book or any one of the others for your area? They aren't cheap are they! However you need to be listed.

I should add at this point that many people, those with smart phones (whether they are smart or not) use these to check the electronic Yellow Pages instead of paper Yellow Pages. And more and more people, young and old, are going to smart phones.

Let's discuss Yellow Pages first. The positive side to Yellow Pages is that the person calling has a real interest in doing business with you and your school. The downside is that all of your competitors are listed there also, so the customer can easily call around.

With the Yellow Pages, size is nice, but is very expensive. The better way to go is a smaller ad, but use a headline, with a benefit and use color to grab the eye to it and to make it stand out. The benefit should be a hook, something to grab them as they read it, once it has caught their eye.

If you want save money, or don't have a lot to spend, then the minimum is to upgrade your free listing to add color to it to make it stand out.

Bottom line is to have a colorful listing without spending too much money.

Now let's talk about web pages. In this day and age, it is a must have for your business. As I mentioned earlier, people are using the internet as their Yellow Pages more and more. This is especially true with smart phones, however, many people like to sit in the comfort of their home and surf the web, so even there, you need a website.

If they have an interest in martial arts and/or self defense, you need to be there to meet their needs.
People use the web not only to find a business, but to get the phone number, hours of operation, address and/or services. Have a website to be there when they search. Join Facebook then setup a business page, get your current customers to join you. Get as many likes as you can. Fact: A number of businesses have built large clientele from social media. Don't lose out.

Do you get it? You need a website AND you need to be on Facebook. Facebook is free and a website should not cost huge bucks. As a matter of fact you probably have someone in one of your classes that can build one or knows someone that does. With that said, your website needs to tout the benefits and convince the reader to come to see you at your school. You make the sale, not the website.

Chapter 9

Advertising: Other

Billboards

When compared to radio, TV and newspapers, billboards can be a bargain. However, for best results you need the high traffic billboards to get the biggest bang for your buck. Your sign needs to be attention grabbing, with few words and BIG FONT. If people are driving fast, it has to be able to be read quickly and yet be informational. If they are driving slower, say 30 or 40 miles per hour, then they are going to be in close traffic, so it has to be able to be read quickly and yet be informational.

The most successful one I saw was built atop the building the school was located in. The school used it two to three months out of the year and rented it out the rest of the time to make money from the billboard.

Bulletin Boards

When money is a factor, bulletin boards at grocery stores, department stores, restaurants and Laundromats are the way to get your name out. Your poster should be done professionally, and landscaped to give you lots of area to show and list benefits, plus gives you a wider area for the tear-off at the bottom. Most people put their phone number on the tear-off. However, what often happens is the person tears off the number and forgets what it was for or worse, they wait and wait then talk themselves out of calling.

To offset this, and one of the reasons why your posters should be done professionally, you need to not put your phone number on the tear-off, but put your school's name and address on it and saying 'Come by for a free session' or something else to get them to come to see YOU at your school. The poster gets them there, you make the sale!

Also, know that many large businesses have bulletin boards for their employees. Ask them to place a poster up with the agreement you will give their employees a discount. A selling point is that healthy employees lower insurance costs.

Advertising Specialties (also known as Promotional Products)

The most common advertising specialty is the ink pen with the company name on it with their address and phone number. Some even have a slogan.

Not only are there thousands of different types of pens and pencils to had, there are tens of thousands of other types of specialty items. Here is just a list of 'C' categories and, like pens, there are usually many types within each category.

' C'

Calculators

Calendar Pads

Calendars

Cameras

Camping Equipment & Accessories

Can Coolers

Candle Holders

Candles

Candy

Candy Machines

Canisters

Cans

Caps & Hats

Carafes

Cards

Cases

Cassette Players

Ceramic Mugs

Chairs

Check Protectors

Cheering Accessories

Chewing Gum

Christmas Decorations

Cigars & Cigar Accessories

Cleaners

Clipboards

Clippers
Clips-Bill
Clips-Pen & Pencil
Clips-Utility
Clocks
Clothing
Coasters
Coin Holders
Coins, Tokens & Medallions
Coloring Books
Combs
Compact Discs
Compasses
Computer Accessories
Containers
Cookware
Coolers
Corkscrews
Cosmetics
Coupon Keepers
Crystal Products
Cups/Mugs
Cushions
Cutters

Don't be overwhelmed, just know that the options are almost endless. With that said there are some things to keep in mind. One is to be careful of the message of what you get sends. An example is a client who purchased cheap pens where his secretary had to test each one before giving it out.

I'm sure these poor quality pens cost him business because they sent the wrong message.

Travel mugs would be more of a gift to your current students as they probably commute to your school. This is a way to say thank you AND put a reminder in front of them to get to class.

However, if you decide to use specialty items to promote your school, then ink pens for sure. Remember to use quality. If you have the potential of contacting anyone in the medical field, make sure your pens have black ink. Although more expensive, the 3-in-1 pen is a hit AND it is one that won't be thrown in a drawer or passed on like so many others. It is an ink pen, with a light and a rubber tip that can be used as a stylus. Not only is it a keeper, it is a pen the owner will talk about. The added bonus is you can give them a 3-in-1 pen you follow up with three benefits of coming to your school.

Whatever you decide to use, pass one out when you give out a brochure. Give one out when they sign a contract with you. You want your name to be seen and this is an excellent way to do so.

Business Cards

Business cards were mentioned earlier, however from an advertising standpoint, bears repeating.
Consider each of these to be a soldier and arm them accordingly. They should match your stationary, however they need to have at least two benefits on them. You might even want to print up cards for each marketing niche you are pursuing. Use both sides. Cards can be powerful! They aren't any more than informational if all they have on them is your school's name, address and phone number. Your competitor's cards are probably like that, right? So dare to be different. Make them work for you. Use them wisely and leave them everywhere!
Put them in every letter you send, even if it is just with the check for your electric bill. You never know what will come from them.

Classified Ads

Yes newspapers were mentioned earlier, however, classifieds are in a place of their own. These work best if you have a community paper. Along with classifieds consider local association and club newsletters as ways to get your name out there.

Where possible use color, it costs a bit more however it makes your ad stand out, really stand out. With these, you need to, when writing yours, use the KISS method (Keep It Short and Simple). Do not quote prices. Do not put your phone number in it, use your address. You want them to come to you.

Choose your section in the classifieds carefully for the market you are going to reach. You might want to place the ad in more than one section or write different ads for different sections and different markets. Try different sections and track your results. Repeat in those that pull the most prospects.

Coupons

Coupons have been mentioned a number of times and with different advertising. Coupons are great if you get them out to enough people. Coupons must have a deadline or they never push people to action. They need to be colorful to attract attention AND they need an attention getting headline that grabs the person's attention and draws them in to read the rest of your coupon. Try different promos to find out what works best for you. Here are a few examples:

A free session when you pay for three.
A free session when you sign up for a year.
20% off the first three sessions.
Come by for a free session (wear sweats)

1/2 hour 1-on-1 training when you sign for 90 days

Note the word FREE is a key grabbing attention word used by copywriters everywhere.

Mailings

There are two ways you can mail to people. One way is to sign up with your local post office to send out mailings. These are very inexpensive and you can pick zip codes or even get as precise as mailing routes. At this time there is a requirement of 1,000 cards per mailing.

There are rules, such as size of the card, how they are printed, type of card stock. They go to every mailbox within your specifications, such as a zip code. These are a great way to promote your business in a specific geographic area.

The second way is to buy a mailing list. There are many companies selling these. However, some have better lists than others. You need to ask how current the list is, if it is a onetime list or if you can reuse it.

The biggest challenge with getting buying a list is what category you want to reach. An example is if you want to get more women you could request a list of women in your area that belong to health clubs. Then send them a letter touting getting fit AND learning how to defend themselves.

I highly recommend you get a professional that can do mail merge to print your letters because this way they can personalize each letter from the name on the mailing list.

You then have to fold the letter and 'stuff' it into an envelope. Address the envelope to the recipient (it should already have your school's name imprinted in the upper left hand corner). Note: You can usually have the person doing the mail merge make you a list of the names and addresses on labels with a sticky back so all you have to do is peel them off and place them on the envelope. The key here is to make your letter personal, give them a coupon with a deadline and make sure it sends a professional appearance.

Summary

Advertising

Yellow Pages: -bigger isn't better, but color
is!
-Use local yellow pages.
-Ask your students which one
they use to pick your best option.

Newspapers: -Use local as much as possible.
-Think classified when money
matters.

Find local directories and newsletters to be listed
in.

TV: -Very expensive, however if you decide
to use it, consider local cable.

Radio: -Can be very expensive, but can be
very effective.

Billboards: -Need to be close to you and
need to be able to be read easily
and quickly.

Bulletin Boards: You can post with something as small as a 3x5 card or go with a landscaped sheet of paper with tear offs at the bottom with your school's name and address. Post these anywhere there is a public bulletin board. Also ask larger local businesses if you can post on their internal employee bulletin boards.

Advertising Specialties (Promotional Items): At the very least buy and pass out ink pens that will promote your school. If you can find a fun item that will send a fun, positive message about your school, go for it.

Coupons: Bright, colorful with attention getting headlines. Remember to put deadlines on them.

Newspaper Inserts: If money matters, these are economical. Make sure they are bright, colorful with attention getting headlines.

Mailings: Two types, one through the post office, sending cards to every mailbox in a certain geographic area. The second is to purchase a mailing list that targets, locally, the group or groups you want to bring in to build your business.

Chapter 10

Connecting to make the sale.

Have you ever connected with someone? That was a trick question. Actually we all connect with some people but not others. Why is that? That is what this section is all about. From surveying and talking to people, to teaching communication skills to student doctors, I've found the words I heard as to why a person chooses and stays with a business like yours is because the owner or the employees Ire people they liked and trusted. There is an abundance of research that supports this. This suggests a connection, or to use a better word, rapport.

Rapport, what is it? How do you get it? Is it worth it? Oh yeah, it's definitely worth it, dollars and sense worth it!!!

Dictionary.com defines rapport as: relation; connection, especially harmonious or sympathetic relation. I like to think of it as being in synch and having the trust of another person.

This next chapters are about how to get it. And is it worth it? **People go to and buy from those they like and trust and they are more loyal to those they like and trust.** That got your attention, didn't it?

People tend to like people who are like themselves. Now that can seem scary, however, hang in here because it gets easier. Think about visiting a foreign country. How much better would you be liked and accepted there if you could speak the language? Instantly and a lot!

Now here is a secret for you: There are 3 basic languages within the English language! When you know which one is dominant for a person, you can speak that language and start building rapport quickly.

Before I go there however, you need to know how to make that work even better. You need to match the person's rate of speech. If they are a fast talker from the east, like New York, you need to speed up your rate of speech. If they are a slow talker, you need to slow down to their speed. You get the idea, right?

Now back to the 3 languages. What you are going to find is that some people are known as visuals, they need to see it to believe it. Some people are auditory, they really hear you. The third group are the kinesthetics, they have to have it feel right and they go with their internal feelings, their instincts.

How do you identify who is using what language? There are two ways. One is the words they use. Visuals use words like: see, clear, hazy, describe, mind's eye, pretty as a picture. Auditorys use words like: hear, listen, sounds, discuss, ringing, tuned in. Kinesthetics use words like: feel, touch, grasp, get a hold of, illustrate.

The second way is to observe eye movement. Visuals tend to look up to the left and or the right, they also tend to defocus when they are thinking. The auditory's eyes move to the left or to the right as if trying to look at their ears and sometimes touch their mouth when speaking. Kinesthetics tend to look downward when they speak and usually they speak more slowly.

Like being left handed or right handed, people use all three modes when communicating, however, it is to your benefit to determine their dominant mode and use their 'language' when talking to them. Within that you match their rate of speech. When you get good at this, you will be able to know when they leave their dominant language and go to another. You will be able to start with a word in that language, then move back to their dominant language and be in rapport.

Within language and rapport, note what words the person uses often, sometimes it might be a phrase. You can tell by **listening to what word or phrase has the most emphasis.** This word, or this phrase, also **has power.** Don't overuse these, however, when making a point or closing the sale, **repeat them back exactly as they were said.**

An example of this is the reason they give you for taking classes. If it is self defense, then you want to emphasize that point more than any other benefit.

Another rapport builder is mirroring and matching. This seems like mimicking, however, it should be done in a way the client doesn't notice.

Mirroring is making the same moves as the person, however using the opposite side. An example would be if the person moves their right arm, you would move your left arm in the same gesture. Matching is using the same body part. When you can do this without the client being aware of it, it is a great rapport builder.

All of this takes practice, however, is well worth it. Tomorrow morning, brush your teeth with your non-dominant hand. Feels different and is a bit uncomfortable, isn't it? Same with doing rapport building, but with time, it will become second nature. Have fun with it!!!

Chapter 11

Towards or away from!

This technique is especially helpful when you are closing the sale. When it comes time to close the sale, to make the deal, it helps to know what motivating direction a person uses. There are two, and a person can be one or the other, or they can be a mixture of both. It behooves you to find out which one the person in front of you is before you try to close the sale, make the deal.

Some people are goal oriented and if that is our personal mode of motivation, we tend to treat everyone that way. These people are looking for the benefits, the rewards, the payoff and work towards the goal that will get them there.

However, there are some folk who are what is known as Away Froms. They understand what a goal is, they just aren't all that motivated by it. For them, it is getting away from something, getting away from pain. As a matter of fact, to motivate them you have to make them feel the pain. Then they get very motivated.

Can you see the power of knowing this when it comes time to close the sale? The question you are asking is, how do you know? How can you tell? It is as easy as asking a question: What do you want from attending? What will having that do for you? Then listen closely to the answer. The goal oriented person will say things like, "I will look and feel good," or, "It will allow me to feel safe in public and get back into a social life." The Away From will say things like, "It will keep me from being bullied," or, "It will keep me from being afraid."

Knowledge is power . . . when you use it!

Chapter 12

How Do They Decide?

How important is it to know how a prospect makes a decision, especially to use your services? I agree; it is very important.

Some people are known as internals, they go inside of themselves to make a decision. Others are externals, and they need outside reinforcement when making decisions. To find out, somewhere in your conversation with the client, you ask, "How do you know when you've done a good job?" For internals, it will usually be they just knew they did a good job. For externals, they were told by someone else. If they use both, go with the one they used first then follow-up with using the other.

How do you use this to close the deal? If they are internal, ask them what they need to know to make a decision. They will tell you.

For the external, you need testimonials, and a live testimonial is even better, however make sure they match the same language, visual, auditory or kinesthetic. It makes a big difference. You can also leverage your expertise and tell them this is the best way to go.

Chapter 13

Let's Process the Process.

What is it with some people who want to know every little detail and ask so many questions you want to run away screaming? There is a reason they are the way they are, it is because they are what is known as specifics. They need, desire and yes crave information and have to have it to decide. The other end of the spectrum are those who are generals, people who like the big picture and are not concerned with the details. And of course, many people fall somewhere in between. Your job is to determine which is more dominant for the person you are talking with.

The way to ask the person is to get them talking about a prior experience like a vacation. Listen to the answer. Specifics will answer with a lot of detail and usually have longer answers. The generals will give a much shorter answer and few, if any, details.

For the specifics, be prepared by having brochures, articles, and a lot of details available for them. They like the information in small chunks and to give them the steps involved. Miss this and you miss the opportunity.

Generals like the big picture and the overall benefits. Too much detail will bore them and you could lose the opportunity.

Once you know their type, the key is to watch the person's body language to make sure you are keeping them engaged in the process as you guide them to the close.

Chapter 14

Is that procedure optional?

Have you ever met a person who was all about the rules and the procedures? You also have met others who like to bend the rules to make things happen. Did you know the first group distrusts the second group? Whereas the rule benders just think the rules and procedure folk are dull and rigid.

The first group is procedure people. When presenting to them you need to give them information in small chunks, step by step (logical steps) and do not overwhelm them with options. Think back to the specifics we discussed earlier. If you are an options person, you might want to consider having a procedure type person help you with your presentation for that type.

The second group are the options people. They like options, they like the why, not the how. They will become bored with the details and like to explore new areas. If you try to give them the same presentation as for the procedure types, you will lose them.

A question you can ask is, "Why did you choose to come here?" A procedure type person will give you the steps and method used. An options person will answer the question with needs and reasons. Listen and if necessary, ask the question again like this: "Why else did you choose to come here?"

Summary

A lot of information for you, a lot of gold, nuggets and gems for you to use. You will not be able to assimilate it all at once and please know it takes time and practice to learn this and to become proficient. However, it is well worth it.

When first meeting a person, you need to quickly learn whether they are visual, audio or kinesthetic and match your words to their type. At the same time you will match their rate of speech. All the while doing a bit of mirroring and matching their movements, but not mimicking, okay?

Watch them to ensure you are building and staying in rapport. Early in the conversation it is easier to ask questions, so as the opportunity arises, insert when you can, some of the questions you were given or that you have made to find out as much information as possible. As you do, start to gear your conversation towards their type(s).

You will need to, as quickly as possible, yet naturally, learn if they are options/procedures, general/specific, because you will lose them quickly if you go down the wrong road.

Are they external? Get your testimonials out and start building yourself up as an expert.

Are they away from? Start telling them horror stories and all the bad things that can happen.

Note: Internals and towards are going to be helping you by their questions and their actions.

So what happens if there is more than one person and they are of different types? You will need to know the other person's types. When talking, when you make eye contact with a person, use their type(s). Also it is a good thing to mix both types of language into your conversation.

As a side note to this, Harvey Mackay in his book, 'Swim With Sharks' has a list of 66 pieces of information his company maintained on their customers and potential customers.

You need to capture this information so you do not have to dig for it each time they come by your school. It behooves you to, at a very minimum, keep note cards on each student to track the information. You can then look these over, check the information prior to their attending so you don't have to start fresh each time or worse, try to go from memory where you might mess up and lose rapport.

You may not need 66 pieces of information, however, more is better when building rapport, connecting with your customers, because knowledge is power!

Chapter 15

Making Your Message!

You have to marvel at the unique lunacy of a language in which your house can burn up as it burns down, in which you fill in a form by filling it out. Or, how about: The present is a good time to present the present.

The English language is strange, isn't it? Yet it is what we work with to communicate. Most teachers, even professors, say you are responsible for 50% of communicating with another person, and the other person is responsible for 50% of the communication.

I do not agree. I see it differently as I feel each person is responsible for 100% of communicating.

Think about it. You send a message and if the other person doesn't get it, who is at fault? Trick question, actually it doesn't matter who is at fault. The key is to not point fingers, but to take ownership and responsibility for ensuring both parties are on the same page, have the same understanding. Makes sense, doesn't it?

You want to make sure you and the other person understand the message you are sending, whether it is verbal or written. I've helped you get a big jump on the verbal, the connecting with the person, now let us consider the written.

Whether you are writing a letter, an email or copy for a brochure or other type of advertising, you want to make sure the message doesn't become misconstrued. However, it isn't as easy as it seems as you have found out. Like when you found out that people speaking the same language, English, speak three different languages within that: visual, auditory and kinesthetic. Now you are finding that the same words can mean different things. Not only that, people can perceive the same message differently because of their different ways at looking at the world.

What follows is not all inclusive, however will help you get a handle on the basics of written communication to include copywriting.

It also gives you some guidance on using questions to garner information and to lead and guide the conversation where you need and want it to go.

Chapter 16

Write, Right or Wrong!

The first rule in writing is one you already know, watch your spelling and grammar. Studies have shown people perceive the intelligence, or even more, place status on how someone writes. It can even effect how they perceive your skills and your ethics. The strangest part of this is even though the person himself or herself might make grammatical and spelling mistakes, the person still judges another person on their writing skills. This is especially true when the person reading has never met the person who did the writing. Sad but true.

There are two ways to overcome this problem. The first is to get a dictionary and a book on grammar like 'The Gregg Reference Manual'. On Amazon, under books, I typed in the word 'grammar', there were over 60,000 hits. Find one that works for you.

Please note there will be times when you might want to make a grammatical error to better promote your business. What do I mean? Don't always use the semicolon between two complete sentences. People reading tend to hesitate at a semicolon. From a copywriting standpoint that isn't always a good thing. If you need them to 'flow' into the second statement, you need to use a comma. If someone should call you on it, apologize and know that person is a 'procedures' and most likely a 'specifics' person.

When writing, especially copy, you need to decide if you are going to write in the active voice or passive voice.

Which of these three sentences do you think involves the reader the most:

1. When someone comes to our school, they leave looking and feeling great.
2. When she left our school she looked and felt great.
3. When you walk out of my school, you will look and feel awesome.

Number 3 because the more you can get the person involved, the better your chances of making a sale.

Another area to remember is around style. To write more lively, vary your sentence structure. Look at ways to alternate how you begin sentences, and combine short sentences to create different sentence lengths. However, avoid overlong sentences unless you are making a statement with it.

What this chapter is talking about is image. The image you present with the verbiage and materials you present to your students and potential studentss. For the same reason you wouldn't wear food stained clothes while training a group, neither would you let unprofessional materials represent your business.

By the way, the second way to have good punctuation and grammar is to hire someone to help you. To get more bang for your buck, hire a copywriter who will not only do the grammar and punctuation, but will ensure you have copy that grabs and sells.

Chapter 17

The Question Point!

'You can lead anyone anywhere with questions.' I think that came from Tom Hopkins, author of 'Selling for Dummies' at one of his Boot Camps for Selling. Questions bring you knowledge, and knowledge is power if used correctly.

Whether speaking or writing, you can use questions to guide, to lead, to focus, demand an answer, uncover facts, keep yourself in control, discern body language. Asking questions can do many things for you!

Asking questions is not interrogating. It is more like a conversation. In the last section I said you need to find an attention grabber to lead your materials for marketing. Questions can do this admirably!

What is even better is to start with an attention grabbing question . . . that you know the answer to, then follow it with a more leading question to direct the person's thoughts in the direction you desire. Your questions in your marketing materials should guide the person to either call your place of business or come there. Those are the only goals of your marketing materials. Too many people try to make the sale in their marketing and advertising. That is wrong because that gives them the opportunity to make the decision whether to buy or not. YOU want to be present when they decide because you will have a ton of information to help guide them to the best decision, the best solution for them.

When in person, continue refining your questions until you have the big picture and any personal issues involved. Remain objective to find the root of the problem as you fashion your questions. Be aware that some people will try to deflect issues by passive aggressiveness, smoke screens or outright lying.

Watch for clues to see if you have triggered an emotion: looks away, widens or narrows eyes, breathing rate changes-faster or slower, folds arms tightly, turns away from you, turns towards you, skin color changes, pupils dilate.

If you perceive the change as negative, you can ask: What are you thinking about? You may or may not get an honest answer, but you will get to see their body languate from the question. Often though, people will respond openly and you gain the exact information you need.

Stay focused. Some people will give you more information than you want or talk about things unrelated to the issue at hand. You can take control by saying, "I understand and . . ." Then lead back to the topic or to the direction you want to go. Another way to change the topic and guide the conversation is to say, "By the way, . . ." and ask your question. Note, you do not want to ask rapid fire questions. As a matter of fact, the conversation should go at the rate of speech of the other person. Using what you learned, you should be in a conversation where you are using questions and your observations to gather the knowledge you need to help the person to the best decision, the best solution in signing up for your school.

To ensure that happens remember to ask the other person questions to ensure understanding on both sides. Unless you check for understanding, you open the door to them leaving, to losing a sale.

Chapter 18

Defining Moments!

It doesn't matter whether you a Martial Arts School, an academy or a self defense school, you need to market and promote yourself, your business. It should be a part of who you are and what you do.

It's a given that some of your customers are going to die or move away. This means, NUMBER ONE: You have to take care of your current customers. Make them the happiest people in the world.

What business are you in? Martial Arts? Self Defense? Yes . . . and no! What you should do, what you must be doing is change your mindset, your attitude and what you see and feel your business is, because if you are doing it right, you are in the making people feel better about themselves business! That's right, your customers should leave looking and feeling better about themselves.

How important is this?   Let me share.   When Harley Davidson, the best branded motorcycle in the world, went public, the president of their company and their leadership fought Wall Street. Wall Street wanted to list them as a motorcycle manufacturer.   Harley Davidson wanted to be known as a 'lifestyle company' because they wanted to be able to do more than sell motorcycles. Not only did Harley Davidson win, they went on to make $40 million dollars from royalties on their name/logo. . . in one year. Yes indeed!!!

Important to know what business you are in?   It will make you dollars and sense!!!

So knowing what business you are in, and then making your current customers happy, happy, happy, then, and only then, market, market, market, sell yourself, sell yourself, sell yourself. Your days go by more quickly when you are busy

AND you will be making more money!

Do it and make positives happen.

Chapter 19

Build It Big!

The Beginning of your journey . . . of who you will
be and what you will have . . .

Do you know why people didn't buy from you?
The main reasons were: they didn't need your
product, they didn't trust you, they didn't have the
money, you didn't show them the benefit of having
your product, they didn't like you, and the worst
reason: they didn't know you exist.

I've written this book to help with all of these
except the first one. Wait you say, what about not
having the money? If you have done your job of
marketing and communicating effectively, and
they see and feel the need, they will more often
than not find a way to buy. And since you are
doing all that has been shown to you in this, your
book, you are on your way to building your
business, building it big!

I am so glad you made it to the end of this, your book. You know, don't you, this is really the beginning of your new life as a new you. You have figured out there is NO reason you cannot achieve your dream.

You've made a strategy, a plan, with all kinds of contingency planning to hurdle any roadblocks so nothing and no one can stop you on your journey and your plan fills you with excitement! Tweak it as you need to so you can stay on track, so you can help others stay on track, okay?

Have you written out your goals and do you keep looking at them morning, noon and night to keep it fresh, to stay focused, to ensure you use all of your resources to your advantage because you have a goal in building your business and you want to see come to fruition? You know what you want and you are willing to make it happen, right?

You've put fun into this because although life isn't always fair, it should be fun, right? Right!!!

You've come to accept yourself as you are, with anticipation of being even better when you move to a higher level in life. It is a good world we have, but will be better when you reach your milestone, then maintain it, don't you agree?

I've enjoyed doing this for you because I care, because I want you to enjoy life and if a part of that is to achieve your dream, your goal, I am glad I could help, I could be a part of your life with these words, these pages. That as you turned each page, this research, this compilation, our baby, 'Marketing Made Easy for Martial Arts & Self Defense: Business Builder and Marketing Manual', (okay your book) increased your knowledge, expanded your horizons and entered you on a journey, on a journey of expectation.

You are on your way, knowing that you can achieve your dream, and please, remember us when you get there. Use this information to maintain your new level in life because achieving your dream is just step one, step two is maintaining, and step three . . . well this is where you get to write your own book, your own life's story. I wish you the very best!!!

Earl O'Kuly

PS: And please remember, you can't fail if you never give up.

Appendix A
Martial Arts Benefits for a Women:

Article from By The Book 4U Publishing, written by: Earl O'Kuly

4 Self-Discipline

Martial arts training will help you to control your inner self and to be in peace. It teaches not only how to be in control of your body but you will learn how to be in control of your mind also. Somewhere in your early sessions, you will start to feel a real calmness in yourself. True martial arts is as much about the mind as it is about the body.

3 Self-Confidence

As you train in martial arts you will find your confidence level increasing. At the end of 90 days, with each new technique you learned, as you feel your body becoming stronger, you will walk out of each session feeling more and more confident, not only in self defense, but more confident in your ability to handle all of the things the world can throw at you.

2 Self Defense

To be able to defend yourself, or to defend a loved one, is one of the basic reasons many people take up martial arts. What you will find is that the more you learn to defend yourself, the less likely you will ever need to use these skills. This is because when you walk in confidence, the less likely you will ever be placed in a situation where you will need to use what you are learning. However, if you do, your mind and your body will come together to allow your skills to manifest.

1 Physically Fit

What is it worth to you to be physically fit? Besides self defense, martial arts makes you focus on your physical fitness as you improve your flexibility, stability, endurance and strength at a faster rate. The more you learn martial arts (and consistently attend sessions) you will see a drastic change in your fitness level as your muscular strength increases and your body becomes more trim, more fit, and more powerful. A lot of people join a martial arts class to attain their goal weight, then stay on because of the many other benefits.

Appendix B

44 more marketing ideas to use to build your strategy, your plan for success:

1. Have a sign prominently posted, **'If you are unhappy with anything, let us know, if you are happy, please let your friends and family know. Thank you!'** Studies have shown that on average when a person is dissatisfied, they tell 7 to 10 people. If they are happy with your work and your service, they tell 2 - 4 people. You want to know if they aren't happy. You want to fix whatever made them unhappy. You want to lose customers only 2 ways: death or moving away.

2. Send out birthday cards - let them know you are thinking of them on their special day. To take this to a higher level, especially if you have only one family member as a student, get the birthdates of the rest of the family and send them a card. PS: Anniversaries are also a good time to send a card.

3. Refrigerator magnets - think about it, how many refrigerators have you seen without a magnet?

Right, not many. There is a magic number in advertising that says people need to see something a certain number of times, like an ad, before they decide to purchase. That number is seven. Now think about how many times they will see your name if it is on their refrigerator. Give these to your students. Put them on a flyer or brochure with rubber cement and pass them out at homes and businesses in your area. Note: it is illegal to place anything in a mailbox without postage.

4. Mailing lists - the mailing list company we contacted had over 200,000 homes with at least one person who was hearing impaired. How many of those are in your area? Check with a reputable mailing list company to find out. Note: there are a few mailing companies that will send your literature for you. Remember the magic number 7? That wouldn't be cost effective, however 3 mailings have a greater impact than one.

5. Flyers - passing out fliers in public places is a good way to get your name out to those who might otherwise not have heard of you and what you have to offer. Staple a business card to the flyer because

often if the person trashes the flyer they will retain your business card. You do like the idea of getting a bit more mileage that way, don't you?

6. Community and school calendars and publications - contact local schools and community organizations to find out what is available. These are usually high visibility at a low cost.

7. Restaurant mats - talk about a captive audience for your business. We even saw a restaurant that sold advertising on the water glasses that not only got the names of the advertisers to the restaurant's customers, but also became the talk of the town.

8. Movie screen advertising - check with your local theaters to find out more about this opportunity. If you use this venue, have colorful, quality material.

9. Post cards - easy to print and a lot less expensive than regular letters. They have other bonuses. First, they can be read by anyone handling them. Second, you reach people who don't open advertising mailings. What announcements, sales or events, can you use these for?

10. Network - join organizations and network, network, network. To make this work, follow-up with notes and thank you cards.

11. New residents - send a welcome package to new residents to your community and follow-up with a phone call. Is there a welcoming organization in your area? If not, you can track new home sales as they are a matter of public record. Also, watch the business section of the newspaper for new employees who are from out of town. Be creative . . . be aggressive!

12. Barter - are there any barter clubs in your area? This a quick way to get new clients. Note: any barter will be considered income, however, when you use your barter it is usually considered a tax deduction so it cancels out AND you get a new customer.

13. Shows and Events - does your community have annual events, parades, home and garden shows, etc? Be there, be colorful, and be inviting.

14. Seminars - offer to do seminars at churches, schools, and local organizations.

15. Customer appreciation parties - hold customer appreciation parties AND have them bring a friend or two. Often the people they bring are similar to themselves.

16. Provide convenience - what can you do to make your business more convenient to your current and prospective clients? Are you open late at least one day a week? Do you offer Saturday hours? Do you accept all major credit cards? Do you accept checks? Do you offer financing? Are you easy to get to/find? People like and appreciate convenience!

17. Run for office - have a popular platform for the majority of the people and show you care. You don't have to care if you win because you are looking to build name recognition and rapport with the people.

18. Write a book - it is not that hard because there are a number of services to help authors, to include

ghost writers. You can use the book as a giveaway, as a promotional item and get publicity from it. What the heck, go for it!!!

19. Set up a wheel of fortune - let customers and the public during special events spin the wheel for fun and silly prizes. Promote this. PS: It is cool to have one for the kids and one for adults.

20. Banners - you've seen them, now let others see yours. Besides in front of your location, be creative as to where else you could place this. Move it around, use it until it wears out.

21. More on billboards - don't forget billboards on buses, trains, park benches, taxis, kiosks, etc. Check them out for price and figure out if it will be profitable, i.e., at least one customer for you.

22. Classified ads - they are cheap and easy. Did you know there are people who read all of these all the time? What nice little classified can you think of to hook some prospects?

23. Newsletter - preferably online, but do both to ensure you meet the needs of your students. This is a good way to stay in touch with your current students and since it is free, any prospects you can send one to. Share information, benefits, events, etc.

24. Coupon mailing services - there are coupon mailing services that can often mail these less expensively than you can. Often the coupons are sent in a packet of coupons and people pull out the ones they are interested in using.

25. Cooperative mailing - get together with other businesses in your area and do a cooperative mailing and share the costs and the cost savings.

26. Coupons - the words FREE and SAVE are attention getters. However, rather than reducing prices, find more creative ways to use coupons. Add a bonus to your products and services and remember to set a deadline to get procrastinators moving. Note: coupons are a great way to get first time clients.

27 Competitor's coupons - check out competitor's coupons and when possible spread the word you will accept the competitor's coupon and add a discount or some other bonus. Don't complain about competition, be better than the competition.

28. BBB/Better Business Bureau - join the Better Business Bureau and you can use their name on your advertising. Don't want to spend the money? Then at least register so people can check there are no complaints about you.

29. Chamber of Commerce - be a member. Often you get to meet newcomers this way. You can network to promote your business. Plus it gives you the image of being a stable, established part of the community. Also, check to see if you can use this in your advertising.

30. Donations - find local not-for-profit organizations that are in need. When possible, rather than money, donate an item that you can get mentioned in the newspaper for publicity. An example would be a food pantry. Setup a food

collection at your site, estimate the weight, and have the local paper send a reporter to capture the delivery.

31. Awards - give awards. An example would be a $200 scholarship to the high school valedictorian. Make sure the local papers are aware of this. Often you can get the school or organization with the recipient make the call to the paper to give the news more clout.

32. Testimonials - if your customers are happy, they will be glad to give them, so use them. Post them prominently in your waiting room. Use them in your brochures and advertisements.

33. Write for local newspapers - talk to a local newspaper about writing articles, especially weekly. If they are not interested, then write a letter to the editor about something in the local news. Remember to keep the tone down, stick to facts and not embarrass yourself. An even better idea is to have a friend write a letter about a good deed you have done.

34. Reprints - when you do get a favorable write-up, take advantage. Post the articles prominently; use excerpts in your advertising; make copies and distribute them . . . everywhere.

35. Newspaper inserts - these are better than newspaper ads in that if a person is interested they keep the insert. Often with an ad, they are interested, but don't cut out the ad and the newspaper gets pitched. Note: you can have a classified that directs them to the insert. Think creatively!

36. Research/stick pins - seeing is believing as the old saying goes. So get a map of your area, place it on a cork board, and stick colored pins in it to show where your current students are coming from. What you are looking for is pocket areas that would be great places to start targeting your business.

37. Be nice to and ask questions of sales reps and suppliers. Make sure they know you want to hear any negatives that are out there so you can make

corrections. They can also share what others in your field are doing to build their businesses.

38. Sales aids - ask your suppliers for free sales aids or for assistance with marketing and advertising. Often they have money, materials and even discounts available just for the asking. Remember to use this wisely with a theme or a special promotion to get the most from your efforts.

39. SBA/Small Business Administration - did you know the SBA has low-cost guides, booklets and brochures for businesses in general and often for specific businesses? Check them out to find out what will work for you to build your business. Note: they also have Small Business Development Centers to help small businesses build their business. They also have S.C.O.R.E., Service Corp of Retired Executives. These counselors are a free service. It is like hiring a consultant for free.

40. Learn from your competition - let your competition do the work for you. Keep a notebook, or actually more like a scrapbook, of your

competitor's advertising. Along with that, cut out and keep advertising and marketing materials that catch your eye. Use this to build your own advertising that is even better. Keep one step ahead and be the best! Ohhh, and another idea around this is to have a friend go to your competitor and when it comes time to buy, have them say they are going to shop around. If appropriate they can even mention they were thinking about coming to you. Now you will know the rest of the story!!!

41. Living testimonials - do you have a customer or two who think you are the greatest because of what you have done for them? Are they personable and articulate? Ask them to be your spokesperson, especially with prospective students. Tell the prospect they do not have to take your word for what you can do for them, while they are sitting there, call your spokesperson and have them tell your prospect how great you are.

42. Famous spokesperson - Did you know that many famous movie stars and athletes will endorse products . . . for a fee? You did know that didn't

you. However, did you know there are A, B, and C levels. The Cs names are those who don't have the pull they once had, however, are still known names. The best thing about them is they cost a fraction of the As. Hmmm, we have you thinking, don't we?

43. Ride in style - get an attention grabbing car. There are antique cars (over 25 years old) and classics (over 20 years old) that are not that expensive, but will make people look, and if you just happen to have a sign on the side with your business name and contact info, let them look. There are also replicas called 'kit cars' that can be had for a good price. Park these in front of your business to grab attention; park them at busy locations, like at a mall; drive it in parades; park it next to your booth at events. Note: We do not recommend corvettes or cars that are showy, but something that is a bit rare and different.

44. Publicity - it is more credible than paid advertising AND even better, it is free! The easiest press release is information that is of interest for a

newspapers business section. Often they will print news of recent training, new employee, retiring employee, anniversary of the business and the like. This also includes new equipment, a new technique, a new product, a new building, a renovation, etc. However, you should be shooting for bigger game. You should have a write-up for any award or scholarship you give out. Note that this type of write-up is better if it comes from a third party. What works for these types of story is to have a hook, something that grabs attention. Is there a success story, even better one where there was a handicap to overcome? How about an interesting hobby? Remember, it doesn't have to be yours, how about one of your employees or students? If you can't get the third party or a friend to make the contact, then you will need to send a press release. These should be short and professional. Note: If it looks and sounds too much like an ad for your business it will not be printed. It is better to not follow-up with a phone call . . . they will call you if there is an interest for more information.

www.ingramcontent.com/pod-product-compliance
Lightning Source LLC
Chambersburg PA
CBHW061334220326
41599CB00026B/5179